Martial Arts

Lauren Robertson

KINGFISHER

Contents

Created for Kingfisher Publications Plc
by Picthall & Gunzi Limited

Author: Lauren Robertson
Consultant: Master Kevin Chan,
Kamon Martial Arts Federation
Editor: Christiane Gunzi
Designer: Floyd Sayers
Illustrator: Roger Stewart

KINGFISHER
Kingfisher Publications Plc,
New Penderel House,
283–288 High Holborn,
London WC1V 7HZ

www.kingfisherpub.com

First published by Kingfisher
Publications Plc 2002

10 9 8 7 6 5 4 3 2 1

ITR/0302/WKT/MAR(MAR)/128KMA

Copyright © Kingfisher
Publications Plc 2002

A CIP catalogue record for this book
is available from the British Library.

ISBN 0 7534 0687 X

Printed in Hong Kong

What are martial arts?

T'ai Chi is a soft style

Karate is a hard style

The martial arts that we know today are based on the ancient ways of fighting from countries such as China and Japan. Most martial arts are now practised as a sport, as a way of keeping fit, or as self-defence. It takes a long time to learn martial arts. They teach students strength and discipline.

Hard and soft styles

There are many different styles of martial arts. They can be divided into 'hard' and 'soft' styles. Hard styles use power, speed and high kicks. Soft styles use slow, flowing moves.

The teacher, or master, has lots of experience

Going to classes

Today, martial arts are taught in special classes all over the world. Students start at the same level and they learn the moves over many years. People who are highly skilled in martial arts are called 'masters'.

4

The Shaolin monks were strong and very fit

Ancient origins

Martial arts started many hundreds of years ago. In Japan, more than 700 years ago, Samurai warriors used Kendo. In China, 1,500 years ago, the Shaolin monks learned Kung Fu. As these arts were taught to other people, many new styles were created. Kung Fu is one of the most famous martial arts and many modern martial arts are based on this.

WARNING!
Martial arts can be dangerous. You must not try the moves in this book unless you have been to martial arts classes.

STUDENTS PRACTISE TOGETHER IN A KARATE CLASS

5

Where in the world?

Many countries, such as China, Japan, Korea, Thailand, India and Brazil, have their own martial arts. People are not sure where and when all the different styles of martial arts began. Some, such as Sumo wrestling, started in China more than 2,000 years ago. Others are quite new, such as Tae Kwon Do, which started in Korea in the 1950s. Today, millions of people study different styles of martial arts around the world.

Kung Fu (China), meaning 'good skill', began in the 6th century. It is now very popular in America and Europe

Brazil

Yin and Yang

Chinese martial arts are some of the oldest. In China, the Yin and Yang symbol is used to show that everything has an opposite, such as black and white. In martial arts, this symbol tells us that both gentleness and strength must be used.

THE SYMBOL FOR YIN AND YANG

Capoeira (Brazil) began in the 17th century

6

Sumo wrestling, the national sport of Japan, began more than 2,000 years ago

Kendo (Japan), meaning 'way of the sword', began in the 14th century

Karate (Okinawa), meaning 'empty hand', began in the 15th century

Judo (Japan), meaning 'the gentle way', began in the 19th century

Tae Kwon Do (Korea), meaning 'way of the foot and fist', began in the 20th century

Japan

Korea

China

Island of Okinawa

India

Thailand

Philippines

Africa

Indonesia

Kalaripayit (India), meaning 'battlefield training', began in ancient India

Thai boxing, the national sport of Thailand, began in the 17th century

Eskrima (Philippines), meaning 'skirmish', began in the 16th century

THIS MAP SHOWS SOME OF THE MARTIAL ARTS PRACTISED AROUND THE WORLD

7

Getting ready

Every martial art has its own kit, but many students wear a white cotton outfit to practise in. All students wear the same clothes to begin with to show that they are all equal. They earn coloured belts as they learn new skills. Each martial art has a different coloured belt for each level.

Students practise in bare feet so that they do not slip

White belts are for new students

Yellow and green belts show that a student has a good range of skills

Brown belts show a high level of skills

What to wear

Students wear loose white trousers and a white cotton jacket called a 'gi'. A coloured belt around the waist holds the jacket in place. Girls also wear a white T-shirt.

Students help each other to stretch before doing martial arts moves

Warming up

Before doing any physical exercise, it is best to do some simple body stretches. This 'warms up' the muscles so that they are ready to do more difficult martial arts moves, such as high kicks and punches.

This leg stretch helps Tae Kwon Do students to do high kicks

Star jumps are a good way to warm up for Judo classes

Twisting sit-ups help to strengthen the muscles

Getting fit

Students of martial arts must be very fit. During a martial arts class students often have to do energetic exercises, such as star jumps and sit-ups, as well as gentle stretches. These exercises help to warm up the muscles, ready for martial arts moves. They also help to build strength.

Sai

Kamma

Tonfa

Jo

Bo

Weapons

Some martial arts use weapons as well as body moves. In Ju-jitsu, the bo, sai, kamma, tonfa and jo are used. All these weapons were used in Japan for fighting hundreds of years ago. Today they are used only for training.

9

Karate

Karate is a Japanese martial art, from the island of Okinawa. In the 15th century, weapons were not allowed on Okinawa, but bandits used them to attack and rob the islanders. To protect themselves, the Okinawans made up a way of fighting using martial arts moves. As this martial art does not use weapons, it is called Karate, which means 'empty hand'.

Karate students must learn to balance on one leg

Karate students are called Karateka

Block

One of the first things to learn in Karate is how to block an attack. This advanced student is using his arm to block his opponent's kick.

High kicks

Karate uses the arms and legs in high-energy punches, strikes and kicks. The kicks are high and powerful. They are used for self-defence, and not to injure an opponent. The boy on the left uses a fast, 'side-thrusting kick', giving his opponent no time to block the kick.

Wrist take down

This move is used in Shotokan Karate and is useful for blocking an attack. The opponent grabs the attacker's hand and twists it to force him to the ground. The aim is to make an opponent submit, but not to hurt him.

The attacker's hand is held until he submits

The punch

For Karate punches, the hand is closed in a fist with the thumb outside the fingers. If it is inside, it may get broken. Students do not punch each other hard. This move is finished when the fist touches the opponent.

Karate chop

One of the most well-known Karate moves is the 'Karate chop'. The edge of the hand is used to strike a powerful blow. This move can be used to block an attack from an opponent. It can also be used by advanced students and masters to break wood or bricks.

11

Ju-jitsu

Ju-jitsu is one of the oldest martial arts from Japan.

The name means 'the soft art', although Ju-jitsu uses many moves such as punches, strikes, kicks, throws, locks and grappling. It is one of the martial arts that was used in Japan more than 700 years ago by the Samurai warriors and the deadly assassins called the Ninja. These people used it for fighting, but today Ju-jitsu is practised as a way of getting fit and for self-defence.

Attacker gets his opponent in a lock by holding his shoulder joint

Ju-jitsu locks

This martial art uses moves called 'joint locks'. A student presses one of his opponent's joints, such as the shoulder or wrist joint. He then forces him towards the floor or mat.

Hojo jutsu

This is a special Ju-jitsu move using a rope. It was used by the Samurai to tie up prisoners. Today it is used by police forces around the world. Do not try to do hojo jutsu at home. Only soldiers and police officers use the hojo rope.

A JAPANESE POLICE OFFICER USING HOJO JUTSU TO RESTRAIN A CRIMINAL

There is a special way to hold the hojo rope

A NINJA LEAPS FROM A TREE TO SURPRISE A TRAVELLER

Ninja assassins
Ninjas used many different martial arts, including Ninjutsu, which means 'the art of stealth'. They were so good at hiding that people thought they could make themselves invisible.

Judo

Judo means 'the gentle way' and it is more a sport than a way of fighting. Judo started in Japan in 1882, and is based on Ju-jitsu. People who practise Judo are known as Judoka. They stand close together and use grappling moves to throw each other on to a mat. Millions of people practise Judo, making it one of the most popular martial arts.

Olympic martial art

Judo was one of the first martial arts taught to women and it is now an Olympic sport. Judo tournaments are called 'shiai'. In shiai, a Judoka scores top points if she holds her opponent on the mat for 30 seconds.

Begin by bowing

Before Judoka start to grapple, they bow to each other as a sign of respect. In competitions, they also bow to the judges.

14

Judo throws

Every Judo move starts with the opponents standing and facing each other. The two Judoka grab hold of each other's 'gi' tightly. Then they use their arms, legs and bodies to try to pull or throw each other off balance.

Judoka grabbing each other's gi

Hips turn quickly

Knees bend

WARNING!
You cannot teach yourself martial arts. Do not try to do these moves until you have attended classes.

1 This Judo throw is known as the 'floating hip'. The attacker takes a step forward with her right foot. She has to turn quickly and move her hip in front of her opponent's body. At the same time, she bends her knees.

Opponent is lifted off the ground

2 The attacker is now in front of her opponent. She straightens her legs, bends her upper body and pushes out her hip to lift her opponent. She swings him over her hip and round to the front in one move.

Attacker keeps her feet on the floor

Attacker is careful not to damage her opponent's wrist

3 The attacker throws her opponent to the ground. She keeps hold of his wrist until he submits, but she is careful not to hurt him. The attacker always lets go of her opponent when he submits. She may hold him down on the floor until he gives in.

Scarf floor hold

Once a Judoka has his opponent on the floor, he will try to keep him there with special Judo holds. For the 'scarf floor' hold, the attacker spreads his legs and leans his upper body on his opponent's chest with his arm around the opponent's neck.

Attacker holds his opponent until he submits

STUDENT LEARNING HOW TO FALL BACKWARDS SAFELY

Both arms are held out in front

As the student leans back, the chin moves towards the chest to stop the head from hitting the floor

Legs fly up in the air

The way to fall

People who study martial arts learn how to fall without hurting themselves. Many moves are done on a soft mat. Students slap the mat with their hands as they fall. The harder they slap, the softer they will land.

Hands slap the floor as hard as they can

17

Kung Fu

Kung Fu is one of the oldest and most famous martial arts. Shaolin monks first learned this art in ancient China. Then these monks taught Kung Fu to other people while on their travels. Gradually, people added new moves and made up their own styles. There are now hundreds of different styles of Kung Fu.

Wing Chun Kung Fu students sometimes train with a wooden dummy to develop their skills

Chinese lion dance

Some Kung Fu schools teach the 'lion dance'. In this ancient Chinese tradition, people dress up in brightly coloured costumes and dance steps that are similar to Kung Fu moves. The lion dance is said to bring good luck.

Wing Chun Kung Fu

Kung Fu has 'hard' and 'soft' styles. The famous martial artist Bruce Lee created a hard style called Jeet Kuen Do. T'ai Chi is a 'soft' Kung Fu style. The most popular Kung Fu is Wing Chun. It was started by a woman in China 270 years ago. It has soft, slow moves as well as hard, powerful punches and kicks.

18

Kung Fu animal styles

The masters who created the Kung Fu styles are said to have copied animals, such as the dragon, tiger and snake. Kung Fu moves can be fast and sweeping, like a snake, or powerful and graceful, like a tiger.

A position in the Dragon style

A position in the Snake style

MARTIAL ARTS STUDENTS PRACTISING KUNG FU ANIMAL MOVES

Kendo

Kendo started in Japan more than 700 years ago. It was a way of sword fighting used by the Samurai warriors and the word Kendo means 'the way of the sword'. Samurai used to fight with swords made of steel – they are the most famous sword fighters in history. Today, people who practise Kendo are called Kendoka. They use swords made of bamboo or wood and do not try to hurt each other. People practise Kendo today to learn patience, co-ordination and self-discipline.

The best swordsmiths
Japanese swordsmiths have been making swords for more than 2,000 years. These swords are made of hard steel, and they are said to be the best in the world.

Ancient warriors
Samurai warriors, or 'bushi', lived a very strict life. They were soldiers who fought wars and punished people who broke the law. They had to be honourable, respectful and obedient to their leaders. The Samurai were fearless fighters who fought many great battles in ancient Japan.

SAMURAI WARRIORS PRACTISING SWORD FIGHTING IN ANCIENT COSTUMES

20

Do

Men

Tare

Tenugui

Kote

Bokken

A KENDOKA
IN FULL KIT

Clothing and equipment

Kendoka wear special clothes to protect themselves. The 'do' guards the chest, and the 'tare' protects the stomach and hips. A 'tenugui' is worn under a 'men', which protects the head. Padded gloves called 'kote' protect the hands. Kendoka use oak swords called bokken and bamboo swords called shinai.

As well as swords, called katana, Samurai used different kinds of spears, or yari

21

Tae Kwon Do

Tae Kwon Do is a way of fighting that is based on Korean kick fighting. It is similar to some ancient martial arts, such as Karate, but it has only been called Tae Kwon Do since the 1950s. The name means the 'way of the foot and fist'. This martial art uses lots of high kicks. Tae Kwon Do kicks are so powerful that they are famous in the martial arts world.

Wood is broken by the kick

Axe kick

Side kick

Famous kicks

To perform Tae Kwon Do kicks, students must learn to balance on one leg. The axe kick and side kick are two of the many powerful Tae Kwon Do kicks. Students of this martial art must learn quickly how to block these moves.

Advanced student has reached black belt level

Knife strike

Flying kick

When she kicks, an advanced Tae Kwon Do student may jump high off the ground and seem to fly through the air. Black belt students and masters can break wood with their kicks.

Back fist strike

Helmet protects the head

Gloves protect the hands

Shoes protect the feet

Knee strike

Special protection

Practise fighting is called 'sparring'. Students of Tae Kwon Do wear special equipment for sparring to protect their heads, hands and feet.

Striking moves

Tae Kwon Do students learn hand, arm and knee strikes as well as kicks. These can be useful when they are fighting close to an opponent.

Thai boxing

The professionals

Thai boxers are very fit and have lots of energy. This sport is hard work, so each boxing match is only five rounds of three minutes each. In Thailand, boys as young as 14 years old compete in boxing matches.

Thai boxing is the national sport of Thailand. It is more a combat sport than a martial art and is also known as 'Muay Thai'. Thai boxing is similar to boxing in the West, except that the feet, elbows and knees can be used as well as the fists to attack an opponent. Thai boxers have to be strong and must be able to punch and kick hard.

Mongkon

Armbands

Padded gloves

Competitor's name

Traditional kit

A Thai boxer often wears a traditional kit. This includes armbands and a headband, called a 'mongkon'. Boxers also wear padded gloves to protect their hands. Their name is printed on their shorts in Thai.

Thai boxers compete in bare feet

25

Sumo wrestling

Sumo is an ancient martial art that began more than 2,000 years ago. It is the national sport of Japan. Sumo wrestlers are large and strong. They fight in a ring called a 'dohyo'. One wrestler has to push his opponent out of the ring or make him touch the floor with any part of his body above the knees. Sumo wrestlers are well paid and highly respected in Japan.

The salt ritual

Before each match, Sumo wrestlers throw salt into the ring. This is called 'the salt ritual'. They believe that it will stop them being injured.

Hataki-komi

Ketaguri

Sumo fighting techniques

In Sumo, pushing, tripping and throwing are used. As with other martial arts, each move has a name. 'Hataki-komi' and 'Uttchari' are used to throw or push an opponent out of the ring. Wrestlers use 'Ketaguri' to trip an opponent. Punches and kicks are not allowed.

Uttchari

26

WRESTLERS USING A SUMO GRAPPLING MOVE

Referee

Wrestlers start each match behind lines marked on the ground

Basho

Six tournaments, called basho, are held every year. A basho lasts for 15 days. Many matches are held each day. Most matches last for only 10 seconds or less.

More martial arts

There are many other martial arts, but not all of them are taught in every part of the world. Some, such as Aikido and T'ai Chi, are very popular but others are only taught in a few countries. Many martial arts started with the same basic moves. New moves were added as the martial arts were taught to more people in different countries.

Kyudo bows are usually taller than the archers who use them

In Aikido, students sometimes wear a long, loose skirt called a hakama to practise in

Kyudo archers draw their bow along the shoulders then fire an arrow up into the air

Aikido

Aikido started in the 20th century and means 'way of harmony'. It is from Japan and uses gentle grappling moves. Students are moving all the time and the moves are graceful.

Kyudo

This is one of the oldest Japanese martial arts. Kyudo means 'way of the bow' and is similar to archery. Kyudo archers fire arrows at a target made of straw.

28

T'ai Chi

This Chinese martial art is said to have started in the 14th century. The name means 'great ultimate fist' but T'ai Chi is a 'soft' style of Kung Fu. It has slow, flowing movements and is thought to keep people fit and healthy. T'ai chi is practised in many countries.

Many people who practise Tai Chi think it will help them to live longer

Many Capoeira moves use only the legs because a slave's hands were often tied together

Savate uses high kicks so students have to have good balance

Savate

This French martial art started in the 19th century. It uses punches and high kicks and is a mixture of boxing and martial arts moves. Today, Savate is a popular sport in some European countries.

Savate gloves are similar to boxing gloves

Capoeira

In the 17th century, African slaves in Brazil invented Capoeira to defend themselves. They made it look like a dance so that their captors would not suspect anything.

29

Watching martial arts

If you would like to learn a martial art, there may be classes in your area. Teachers may allow you to watch the class before you join. Some martial arts have tournaments or events that people can go to see and there are special shows that people can watch. There are also many martial arts films, starring actors such as Bruce Lee and Jackie Chan.

Sporting tournaments
Karate and Kendo tournaments can be exciting to watch. Judo and Tae Kwon Do are Olympic sports that are shown on television worldwide.

Martial arts show
Shaolin monks are said to have learned martial arts in China 1,500 years ago. Today, Shaolin monks travel the world and put on a thrilling show of their martial arts skills. The show includes high leaps, kicks, flying through the air, breaking sticks and bricks, and other dangerous stunts.

Glossary

archery The art of shooting with a bow and arrow.

assassin A person who is paid to kill people.

axe kick A Tae Kwon Do kick. The foot is thrust above an opponent's head before dropping like an axe.

block To stop an attacker from striking one's body.

captor Someone who holds people against their will.

flexibility The ability to bend easily.

flying kick A Tae Kwon Do kick made with both feet.

gi A white cotton jacket worn for many martial arts.

grappling Martial arts moves where two people work closely together using locks, holds and throws.

hard style Martial arts that use speed and high, powerful kicks.

hojo jutsu A special Ju-jitsu move that uses a rope.

hold Any move used to keep an opponent still.

Judoka People who practise the martial art of Judo.

joint lock A way to hold an opponent still by pressing on a joint in the body. A joint is where a bone is attached to another bone, such as at the knee and wrist.

Karate chop A powerful blow struck with the edge of the hand that can break wood or bricks.

Karateka People who practise the art of Karate.

Kendo A martial art from Japan using a sword.

Kendoka People who practise the art of Kendo.

martial artist A person who practises one of the many martial arts.

master A person who is highly skilled in martial arts.

Ninjas Japanese men who were good at hiding and were paid to kill people.

opponent A person who fights against another in a martial art or other sport.

Samurai Sword fighters who lived in ancient Japan.

Shaolin monks Chinese monks who first used martial arts 1,500 years ago.

side-thrusting kick A Karate kick where the body is turned sideways and the foot is thrust out.

soft style Martial arts that use slow, flowing moves.

sparring To practise martial arts or fighting wearing special equipment.

strike Any blow to an opponent's body using the hands, arms or knees.

submit To give in.

Index